BUILD AUTHORITY FAST!

Grow Your Business with Booklets

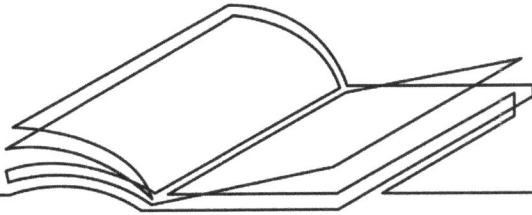

CHRIS O'BYRNE

ISBN: 978-1-64184-044-6 (paperback)
JETLAUNCH.net

CONTENTS

SPECIAL OFFERS
JUST FOR YOU

Ready to jump in and do it yourself? Then you *must* get my course:

Write a Booklet and Build Authority

jetlaunchbooklets.com/course

To schedule a strategy session with me where we analyze and determine the best book or booklet for you, go to **https://bookme.name/jetlaunch/30**

Finally, my Facebook group:

Make Money with Books and Booklets

has tons of informational videos and a vibrant community of business builders like you.

facebook.com/groups/buildauthority

A MAN NAMED BOB

To anyone seeking success in this bold new world thrust upon us by the Internet, we need to have an honest, frank talk. You see, what appears on the surface rarely shows what's really going on. All too often, we just keep passing along what we think is the truth because "that's how it's always been done." It's all meant with the best of intentions, of course, but rarely do things change until someone has the courage to question the standard.

If we approach this fascinating new world with the same methods of the old, we're doomed to repeat the failures of the past, never understanding the joys we can experience with these wonderful new tools available to us. Yet, to ignore where we've come from is to throw away a vast knowledge base from which we can also find the fastest route to our potential success.

What is in your hands is a guide to help you take advantage of "the best of both worlds" (for lack of a better phrase) and begins with the story of Bob. His name could just as easily be Mark, Sue, John, Gertrude, or Barnabas Templeton Jones. But today, we're sharing Bob's story. You've undoubtedly met Bob before and may find many parts of his story familiar. Probably because you've lived them.

Like so many other generations of kids, Bob was sold on the idea that success and college went hand-in-hand and anything outside of that was guaranteed failure. It's true that many people have found their happiness in life this way, and our intrepid hero set his sights on his college degree.

Bob flat-out loved the experience of meeting so many new people, eager to set out into the world after escaping the clutches of his parents who clearly didn't know as much as he did. Several hangovers later, he took a few steps across a stage to shake the chancellor's hand while wearing a ridiculous looking hat and walked off with his magical piece of paper into "the real world."

Bob had taken care of everything he needed to partake in this mystical world of promise and grandeur that he dreamt of for so many years. Along came the first "real" job with a paycheck that had more than three digits before the period.

Then a sweet new ride.

And a mortgage.

And then a letter from the Feds saying they wanted all that loan money back.

The lights weren't as bright and shiny as he was told they would be. That's okay, though. Bob was in the "real world," working hard, and at least the bills were getting paid. He still had that glorious 48 hours every weekend to himself to rest up before the alarm went off again on Monday morning. And, if he continued to work hard, he might be up for that promotion, soon.

Which he indeed got! Yet the prices of groceries and the gas for his sweet ride kept going up, pretty much wiping out the increased pay he received. And those darn Feds were still rather persistent about getting their money back for all of those hangovers—uh, the education he got.

This went on for quite a few years until Bob started asking questions about the story he'd been sold for so long. Was this really it? An endless routine of alarm clocks and working late for a boss who was more interested in his performance than him? His pay raises barely covering the increasing cost of living? All this so he could retire in 40 years on a third of what he was making?

Bob swallowed that tough pill and realized something had to change to get out of this cycle of madness. He started paying more attention to this whole "side hustle" thing he'd read about on Facebook. What could be so hard about becoming an entrepreneur, right? (Aside from remembering how to spell it, of course.)

So, instead of spending evenings catching up on the news or going out with his friends (who all now started calling him crazy, anyway), Bob went into business for himself. He put in the work until one day he walked into his boss's office and said, "I quit!" He was, at last, a full-time business owner with a bright-looking future once again.

But it's never really that easy, is it? Customers don't just come knocking on your door. And if the advertising isn't working as planned, just buy more of it, right?

Yet, no matter what happened, all those courses he took on Facebook ads, how to leverage Instagram and LinkedIn, creating an endless stream of content, going to conferences and masterminds and networking, building relationships and filling his bookshelves with the countless notebooks and more courses he bought…

Nothing would scale. Sure, he was doing okay and didn't have to go crawling back to his boss, but it wasn't enough. Where was the success he was promised so many times? Why was it still eluding him no matter what new strategy or shiny object he tried? Why was he still struggling?

This is where Bob's story takes a shift. Bob came and shook my hand after I spoke at an event about the power of booklets to build your business. He wasn't very optimistic at first about what they might do for him, but he figured what's the harm in one more attempt after the dozens of strategies he'd already tried.

The cool thing was that he already had all of that content he had created for his blog, Facebook posts, and LinkedIn articles. So, he sent them off to my team at JETLAUNCH to edit and turn into a booklet.

Less than a month later, Bob had a physical booklet in his hand and started selling them on Amazon. He also sold them on his website with a free + shipping sales funnel. Within months, Bob had new customers pouring into his business. So many, in fact, that he had to hire his first assistant to keep things running smoothly. Then another. And then another!

Within a year, he tripled his business and finally reached what he thought was success. He realized that success isn't so much a destination as it is a journey and goals are just stepping stones along the way to keep propelling us forward. Instead of retiring, he set his sights even higher, had two more booklets created, and his future looks brighter than ever.

I've helped several Bobs along the way. I've also helped Mark, Sue, John, Gertrude, and Barnabas Templeton Jones. They've all asked me why a simple booklet had such tremendous power to turn their businesses around and bring them the success they had always desired.

You're about to learn what I shared with them.

YOU NEED TO BUILD AUTHORITY TO BE SUCCESSFUL

So here's the catch-22 in which we often find ourselves: You need to have authority to be successful online, yet everyone in this arena is also seeking to be an "influencer." It creates a lot of noise, and we often find ourselves trying to yell louder than our counterparts just to be heard. That can make it challenging to stand out, and then we drink a lot more tea to soothe our throats. The tea companies love it, but I digress.

We've always had influencers in our lives. Publicly, we call them celebrities, politicians, newscasters, or even authors who write books or for newspapers or magazines. Privately, they can be our parents, grandparents, or maybe even teachers or clergy.

While we might think influencers require millions of followers, this comparison demonstrates that's not the case. We only need a following of people interested in what we have to say. We build our authority by demonstrating our expertise on our particular topic, and as we gain the trust of our audience, our authority expands.

Teaching is perhaps the greatest way for us to expand our authority. However, if we only ever teach in person, we place a hard limit on our circle of influence. We need a way to teach around the clock, regardless of where people live, so that we only have to teach once, but our lessons live on indefinitely.

That's where social media can make for such a powerful tool. But how do we overcome that challenge of trying to be heard in all that noise before we do have our millions of followers and money like Oprah?

You're holding it in your hands!

MY EPIPHANY ABOUT BOOKLETS

As a quick side note, it's important that anything you write speaks directly to the benefit of your reader. They're generally interested in what they can gain from your knowledge and experience and not nearly so much about you.

However, there are also times we have to speak about ourselves to help establish the point we wish to make. This is one of those times.

I've long known that writing and publishing a book is a great way to build authority and make a lot of money. We see plenty of examples of people doing that and Russell Brunson is an excellent example of this. ClickFunnels is a brilliant software platform, but it didn't find the incredible success it deserved until Russell started publishing books that established his authority on marketing.

However, books can be hard to write and take a long time. And how many people do you know that have the time to consume large books regularly? Of course, they're worth the time invested, but check this out:

I was ordering a booklet from Grant Cardone one day called The Millionaire Booklet: How to Get Super Rich when it hit me. A booklet is very easy to read, and most people already have enough content to create one or two (or more) booklets. But the next thought that hit me was even more powerful: A booklet is even more effective than a book!

You see, most people buy books and then only consume maybe a few chapters at most if any of it at all. But a booklet is laser-focused on one very important topic, is easy to consume (often in just minutes), and delivers a powerful message that can improve someone's life. Not only is the message delivered rapidly, the reader feels the psychological effect of feeling better for having accomplished something they don't often do. These good feelings get transferred to the author and poof—the author has generated the authority they are seeking.

When we craft the booklet correctly, the readers are interested in learning more about the author (whose information is conveniently in the back of the booklet), they go to the website, and then sign up for more.

A book doesn't always provide this kind of experience. Readers will more often feel let down and upset with themselves for having not completed the book. Human nature suggests we tend to transfer those feelings to the author and then won't even look to see what the offer is at the end.

Which of these experiences would you prefer your potential customers have?

Can you still write a book?

Of course! Books are still effective and have their place in branding and marketing. Sometimes, we do need to use a full-length book to fully deliver the message we need.

However, consider creating a series of booklets and then combining them into a book later down the road. Each booklet can be a chapter in your book, and then you add an introduction and conclusion to finish it off.

It's a faster, more effective way of creating authority, and you can leverage the branding and marketing power that comes with each booklet for the book as well.

You can also collaborate with other authors, each of you creating a booklet to then use as a chapter of a book. Charge them for the service, and suddenly you've paid for your own booklet and book while building valuable relationships while everyone leverages everyone else's audiences.

Creating books in this fashion can often be a more effective method of creating powerful relationships with other influencers than it is for reaching your potential customers. After all, the influencers you establish relationships with are influencing your potential customers.

HOW TO BUILD
AUTHORITY FAST

With increased authority comes increased business.

We want to connect with people and hear their stories. It's how we relate to one another and find our common ground. When we want others to connect with and learn from us, we do that by offering a glimpse into our own lives.

This is why we are constantly hammered by so much content on social media in the form of video, audio, photos, blogs, advertorials, tweets, Facebook Lives... (certainly there's more, but you get the point) The general idea is that when you post enough content, you'll eventually get enough attention, and your authority will come. You could spend every waking moment creating more content. Many do, and it's wonder they ever sleep!

Let's compare this again to the power of creating a book or booklet. We already mentioned Russell Brunson. Let's also add Tony Robbins,

Lewis Howes, Brendon Burchard, Grant Cardone, [insert your personal favorite], and we create a list of remarkable influencers that stepped up their game through the power of the written word. Yes, they've done other work to increase their influence, but it was their books that put them on the map.

Think about it: Creating a book or booklet requires the distilling of tremendous skill and experience. For example, consuming Brendon Burchard's book High Performance Habits is like taking a semester-long course on high performance. Reading Lewis Howe's booklet The Millionaire Morning is like spending a weekend with Lewis himself.

Further, there's a visceral feeling of literally holding something in your hands. It makes for a more personal experience as opposed to reading a message on a screen. Paper takes on a life of its own when graced with our knowledge.

Your booklet might only have the amount of words as a handful of long Facebook posts, but when we combine the power the above, the impact is far more powerful. Social media posts take a while to build up in your system and require constant attention lest the reader forget about you and move on to the next influencer (or cat video).

A booklet, though… It's like getting several months' worth of the benefits of social media posts in one big shot. It carries more weight and can form the basis for many social media posts so that you can get the benefits of both.

Better yet, the effect of the booklets continues to work, even if they're not being read. Social media posts drop away from people's attention, yet we store written materials on furniture specifically designed for their storage. Or instead of trying to be fancy here, we could just call it a bookshelf.

Even if we never read what we've picked up, it sits there reminding us there is value in those pages. Good luck trying to get that kind of influence with social media.

GET PAID TO WRITE YOUR BOOKLET

Getting paid to write a book is often associated with well-known authors working with traditional publishers who advance them a part of their royalties so they can afford to eat while they lock themselves in a closet for weeks on end attempting to meet a deadline. That certainly still happens for a few authors, but there's another way that's much more accessible to the rest of us. In fact, you can make much more money with it than a traditional publisher, enough that you could create a highly profitable side income or revenue stream.

If You're a Speaker

Most speakers start their career by talking about whatever topic they believe they have expertise in. At some point, many think if they had a book they could sell it from stage, earn more money, and get more speaking engagements. They are indeed correct, but then they realize sitting down to write a book is a long and arduous task for most people.

What they often don't realize is that the talks they've given are perfect for booklets! You can have your talks transcribed into booklets (often with little to no editing) and sell them at events (or through Amazon or their websites using a free plus shipping funnel), build their brand accordingly, get more speaking gigs then you know what to do with, and explode your business.

It's more about redirecting where you put your efforts than piling on a huge additional workload. The best speakers have already put tremendous time and effort into writing and delivering their talks. They also often have several talks practiced and ready to sell to companies or organizations. If you're a speaker, you probably already know the wisdom of video recording all of your talks so you can master the subtleties of the message you're delivering. Recording them gives you a variety of talks that you can have transcribed into booklets you can use for powerful lead magnets. They also give you the basis for that book you've wanted to write, just like we talked about in the last chapter. We'll cover more on this later.

If You're Already Teaching

You may already be teaching. Maybe it's a course or a class or getting in front of others in some form or fashion either live or online. You're delivering valuable information. All of those materials you've gathered and created are perfect material for your booklets. You've already done the work, and now it's just a matter of organizing the information.

The same is true for any blog posts you've written, videos you've recorded, or anything you've created for your social media platforms. It's literally sitting right there, ready to be reorganized, and just like that, you'll have your first booklet. In fact, most people reading this probably already have enough material to create a whole stack of booklets. We just need to take the time to assemble them into booklet form.

If You Have No Content

For those of you who don't have content, there's no reason to panic. Just because you've not written or recorded anything, let alone know what to talk about, that doesn't mean you don't have expertise.

In fact, creating your first booklet could be the ideal exercise for you to get yourself organized, create valuable marketing materials, and establish authority in one fell swoop.

Please pardon me as I talk about myself again for a few paragraphs...

I've been running a book design business for many years and have done quite well at it. We've experienced exceptional growth over the past four years, and it's continuing to grow faster and faster. I've done a bit of my own writing and video work, but not to any great extent, and certainly not enough to readily turn into a booklet, let alone a book. However, I have a lot of knowledge about the book industry, especially about self-publishing, marketing books, and using them to build brands and businesses. That knowledge is ripe to deliver in some form and then turn into booklets.

My first booklet was created from an interview an influencer did with me on a Facebook Live. I took that 45 minutes of talking, had it transcribed, put my editing cap on (I'm a professional at this), had it designed by my company, and boom—I had a booklet.

For my next few booklets, including this one, I wrote a list of several topics in which I have expertise and talked to others about it informally either by phone or email. I know I could talk even more about these topics because I have a bunch of information just sitting there in my head ready to be delivered in audio or written form so I could turn it into a book.

On a long drive I recently made to a mastermind I was speaking at, I wrote, via voice recording, a book about the free plus shipping method for selling tons of books. I had it transcribed, edited, and then turned that into another booklet. I did the same with the talk I gave at the mastermind, which means I created three booklets in one weekend, two of which came from recording myself as I drove.

People take creating booklets too seriously!

How easy would it be for you to create a list of all of the topics you already know a lot about and then turn those into a booklet? I dare suggest you could easily create 50 booklets over a year's time that you could then combine into full-length books. If we figure it takes 10 booklets to create one book, that would be 5 full-length books you've written—in one year!

It's amazing how productive you can be when you know the right techniques and leverage the work of other people. In my case, I'm leveraging the work of JETLAUNCH.net, my own company, to design the books for me. I hire someone, again within my own company, to do ads on Amazon, then have another person create a book funnel for me, one for each of these booklets. I can upsell the recorded audio, the recorded video if I've created one, or additional booklets and sell them as a bundle. There are no limits to what you can do with this.

GETTING PAID TO TEACH

Let's dig deeper into getting paid upfront to write our booklets. The next step is to create a course or series of courses to teach live and as an online course. It's pretty easy to create a group coaching program based on all the materials you've created and turned into booklets. These are just an extension of the work you've already done. The income you get from your coaching program is many times more than you'll ever earn with a traditional publisher earning maybe 8% in royalties.

For your course series, you want to come up with a list of seven to ten topics you can spend about an hour talking about. You'll note this matches perfectly with the work you've already done in the last chapter. Add another hour for questions and answers. These Q&A sessions provide invaluable feedback as you find out where people need more clarification, which, in turn, allows you to perfect what you're teaching. Further, you'll find additional topics this way that you can turn into more booklets and courses.

It might sound like a lot, but an hour can fly by pretty fast, especially when it's a topic you're familiar with. Accordingly, it's wise to have it planned out and practice ahead of time. Keeping a list in front of you of your main talking points is super helpful. Also, storytelling is a powerful tool, so be sure to include anecdotes, stories, and other examples to emphasize your key points.

Before going any further: Please don't feel that your presentation needs to be perfect! You're teaching a class, and it will be interactive. Practice will indeed help you get better, but people are more interested in you being real, and nobody is going to keep track of your "ums" or stutters. They will overlook all of that as long as you're sharing real value that people can learn from.

It's okay to be more casual and conversational. Think of it as talking with your friends. Do you ever complain that your friends aren't super polished or provide the perfect delivery when you're having a conversation? People want to connect with you, and this is more about teaching than it is about giving a polished presentation. Obviously, we want to practice, but with enough time, you're going to get very good at this, and it will all flow more naturally.

The next step is to pick where you will hold your class. The best option is to deliver the class in person because a live workshop carries significantly more weight, even if it's just a short, two-hour workshop. The more people value you what you teach them, the more you can charge, up to $100 or $200, to hear you talk in person.

You're also wise to video-record the entire thing. And before you run out thinking you need to buy or rent thousands of dollars worth of cameras and lights, know that I use my iPhone and a remote microphone that I spent about $70 for on Amazon. The remote mic frees me to walk around, so I don't have to worry about where the phone is placed in order to pick up my voice.

Of course, you can spend more money if you want to, and maybe you've already have some camera equipment you can use. The point is that you don't have to feel limited by equipment because there are many good options readily and cheaply available.

As far as locations go, there are again many options. Perhaps it's the living room of someone's large home or maybe even a dining room is enough space if it's a small group. Many libraries have private rooms available, and there are many other companies whose business is to rent rooms. Heck, the electric company in my hometown rents rooms for cheap. It might take a little bit of research on the Internet, but there are all kinds of options available.

If it's a larger group, try renting a conference room or even bigger. Many hotels have these available, which will also give you the option of booking a room for a night or two so you can rest before and after you give the class. This is perfect if you're teaching out of town, and renting a conference room in a hotel near the airport can save you from even having to rent a car.

And let's not forget we live in the age of Airbnb. There are plenty of large houses available to host your events and give you a chance to try out living in a mansion for a few days. You could even add that as an upsell to a select few to stay at the mansion and get more one-on-one time with you.

In case it's not been stated clearly enough—the options are limitless!

With this done, you've accomplished the hardest

part. You've got your series of talks planned, the location where you're going to share them, and the equipment to record them. All you have to do now is give the talks, record them, have them transcribed, and turn them into a booklet.

This is where the fun begins! Let's talk about how much you money you can make just from creating your booklet. (Before you actually sell it or use it to generate leads.)

HOW MUCH CAN I GET PAID?

That's the underlying question, isn't it?

Check this out:

Let's say you charge $100 for a two-hour session. (You'll get to charge more later, but right now we want to get you started) People will pay that because they want to learn something that's highly valuable to them. Let's say you get 30 people to attend; that will yield you $3,000 per class you teach.

You might even find that you enjoy this process and decide to do it again. As your authority expands, you'll find you can do it without much traveling if you go to local or regional cities. Most people live fairly close to big cities with populations of at least one hundred thousand people or more, which is more than enough to get plenty of people to come to your presentation.

Now, say you teach this course once a month. You're making $36,000/year while doing relatively little work because you've already created your presentation, and all you have to do is show up and talk to people. It's pretty fun!

Let's take it one step further. If you teach two different classes (to create two different booklets), you can double your income to $72,000. You can even teach both classes on the same day. And if you teach four different classes (two on Saturday, two on Sunday, for example), you're now earning $144,000/year. Are the wheels turning, yet?

ADDITIONAL WAYS TO EARN MONEY

You are also to make money in several other ways. When you set up your sales page for people to sign up to attend your talk, add an upsell option to your sales funnel for people to purchase the video recording of the talk they will be attending. If even 10 people pay $197 for it, you've added a few thousand dollars to your pocket for something you were going to do anyway. They will find tremendous value in the video because they know they can go back and review what they heard after they've attended your workshop. Taking enough notes at a live event is difficult to do, and this way they can be much more relaxed while they're there, which provides even more value.

Remember, too, that you're turning this talk into a booklet. They can pre-order the booklet for $20 just for the privilege of being the first ones to receive it.

You can also extract the audio from your talk and turn it into an audiobook. Or record yourself reading the edited version of your booklet using some better audio equipment. You can sell these directly to your customers, and also put it up on Amazon/Audible and get more sales, not to mention reaching a bigger audience.

You can also consider upselling a personal one-on-one session with you. People are already attending your presentation and buying your materials because they are interested in what you know. Some of them will pay good money to have you dig into the details of their business and create a highly personalized strategy to help them succeed. These personalized sessions can easily sell for $500 to $2,000, depending on your market and the return they can expect from your offer.

As you can see, there are many additional revenue streams you can develop just from your booklets and your talks. This is a much more profitable path than simply counting on advances of royalties the way traditional authors typically get paid. You'll note that it's also much easier once you know the path, and it puts you miles ahead of your competition.

CREATE YOUR MMM
(MASSIVE MARKETING MACHINE)

The best part of the video recording process is how you're going to use these recordings to create massive amounts of marketing materials. You can use them to sell your courses, get people to go to your talks, sell your booklets, and sell your services. Even if you own a business that is not based on doing talks and teaching courses, you can use them to generate serious leads for your business.

It begins with massively repurposing your video. We've already mentioned using the video as an upsell to people who come to see you talk. You can also split that video into pieces and use those on your various social media platforms like Instagram, Instagram TV, YouTube, Facebook, Facebook Live, and LinkedIn. There are many places you can use your video and can even break it up into a series of shorter clips.

For example, a 2-hour talk would yield 12 ten-minute clips. There are many video courses composed of clips of that length. You could turn that into a paid course you could sell through your website or other platforms like Udemy, Thinkific, or Teachable, among others.

You can also take photo clips from your video, particularly of you actively teaching or explaining something. Combine them with good quotations, and now you have Instagram posts. These are very popular and good for building your Instagram profile, which you can in turn use to leverage and use to sell more books and more courses and build your mailing lists.

You also have all of your written material to repurpose. You can split your manuscript into multiple blog posts, many Facebook posts, articles on LinkedIn, or even one longer article you can post on Medium. All of your written material is super valuable, and you can distribute these clips everywhere.

You now have a butt-load of video, photos, audio, and written material. Combine your creativity with a little bit of thought and effort, and you'll come up with many more ways that you could use these materials.

Just by creating these courses and recording them, you have created an MMM that will bring you lots of money, JETLAUNCH your brand, and explode your business. It will blow your mind how effective a widespread content marketing system like this will build your brand and business for you.

A Word Of Warning

Professional editing is crucial, and if you don't intend to use it, there is little point in even bothering with any of this work. Poorly transcribed manuscripts come off badly, as do poorly designed and edited booklets. Instead of helping you, they will actually hurt your brand, and you will lose business. Professional services don't cost all that much and will make the difference in helping you look like the professional you actually are. This is not the place to skimp. Besides, what you make from teaching one class will pay for all of the expenses related to creating your booklet, including a professional edit.

CREATE AN ENTIRELY NEW BUSINESS

What you have just read is more than enough to help you create an entirely new business! You could drop whatever it is you're doing, do only this, and live very comfortably from one series of courses. Each year you could create another course, another series of classes that you teach, and repeat the process all over again. Perhaps you keep doing the first one, and now you have a second, and maybe even a third. Take it as far as you like and see how much you can build your brand and your income.

Remember, this is the exact method that many of the big names have used to build their own brands and businesses. We're talking people like Tony Robbins, Brendon Burchard, Lewis Howes, Gary Vaynerchuk, Grant Cardone, Ed Mylett, Russell Brunson... the list goes on.

Many people have done this very same thing where they leveraged their books, their materials from creating those books, got paid to create those books in the first place, and then went on to have massive speaking engagements, coaching programs, and live events. Just look at the events that any of those listed authors have hosted. They're truly incredible.

They started from the same place you're at right now. They weren't experts, but they had knowledge and expertise. They learned along the way, leveraged what they knew into books and booklets and creating courses, and put in the effort to come up with something helpful and valuable. You now have the knowledge to become just like them, enjoying the same kind of success they have, simply by following the method you're holding in your hands right now.

The real question is—what are you going to do with it?

SPECIAL OFFERS
JUST FOR YOU

Ready to jump in and do it yourself? Then you *must* get my course:

Write a Booklet and Build Authority

jetlaunchbooklets.com/course

To schedule a strategy session with me where we analyze and determine the best book or booklet for you, go to **https://bookme.name/jetlaunch/30**

Finally, my Facebook group:

Make Money with Books and Booklets

has tons of informational videos and a vibrant community of business builders like you.

facebook.com/groups/buildauthority

ABOUT THE AUTHOR

A former chemical engineer and high school teacher, Chris O'Byrne built JETLAUNCH.net into the premier book and booklet company for entrepreneurs, speakers, coaches, and consultants.

Chris now travels the world teaching people like you how to write and publish a booklet in one week or less.

Your expert booklet will generate tons of leads and position you as an authority.

Build your brand; build your business.

JETLAUNCH.net has been used by successful entrepreneurs and authors like John Lee Dumas, Ed Mylett, James Smiley, Dan Norris, Charlie Gilkey, Jim Hunter, Kary Oberbrunner, and members of Lewis Howes' Inner Circle.

SPECIAL OFFERS
JUST FOR YOU

Ready to jump in and do it yourself? Then you *must* get my course:

Write a Booklet and Build Authority

jetlaunchbooklets.com/course

To schedule a strategy session with me where we analyze and determine the best book or booklet for you, go to **https://bookme.name/jetlaunch/30**

Finally, my Facebook group:

Make Money with Books and Booklets

has tons of informational videos and a vibrant community of business builders like you.

facebook.com/groups/buildauthority